A Taste of Culture

Foods of France

Peggy J. Parks

KIDHAVEN PRESS
A part of Gale, Cengage Learning

GALE
CENGAGE Learning

Detroit • New York • San Francisco • New Haven, Conn • Waterville, Maine • London

© 2006 by KidHaven Press, a part of Gale, Cengage Learning

For more information, contact
KidHaven Press
27500 Drake Rd.
Farmington Hills, MI 48331-3535
Or you can visit our Internet site at gale.cengage.com

LIBRARY OF CONGRESS CATALOGING-IN-PUBLICATION DATA

Parks, Peggy J., 1951–
  Foods of France / by Peggy J. Parks.
    p. cm. — (Taste of culture)
  Includes bibliographical references and index.
  ISBN 0-7377-3032-3 (hardcover : alk. paper)
  1. Cookery, French—Juvenile literature. 2. France—Social life and customs—Juvenile literature. I. Title. II. Series.
  TX719.P364 2006
  641.5944—dc22
                                                    2005007154

Printed in the United States of America
4 5 6 7 12 11 10 09 08

Contents

Chapter 1
A Passion for Food   4

Chapter 2
Bon Appétit!   18

Chapter 3
Delicious Desserts   31

Chapter 4
Foods for Celebrating   43

Metric Conversions   55

Notes   56

Glossary   58

For Further Exploration   60

Index   61

Picture Credits   63

About the Author   64

Chapter 1

A Passion for Food

For the people of France, food is one of life's greatest pleasures. The French are passionate about good food. They savor everything that is served at a meal, from crusty bread and creamy cheeses to rich, delicious desserts. Just as important as the food itself is the time spent talking and laughing with family and friends. Nutritionist Françoise L'Hermite explains this: "For France, a meal is a very particular moment, in which you share pleasure, the food as well as the conversation. . . . If you have no pleasure in it, you are breaking all the rules of eating."[1]

Many people consider French cooking, or cuisine, to be the most delicious food in the world. There is no one style of French cuisine, however. France is divided into

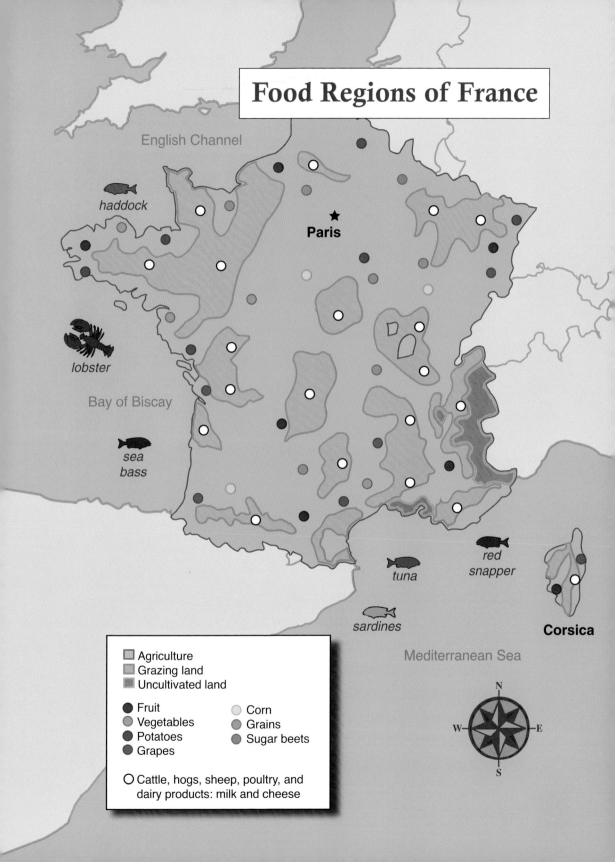

Food Regions of France

English Channel

haddock

lobster

Bay of Biscay

sea bass

★ **Paris**

tuna

red snapper

sardines

Corsica

Mediterranean Sea

Agriculture
Grazing land
Uncultivated land

● Fruit
● Vegetables
● Potatoes
● Grapes

○ Corn
● Grains
● Sugar beets

○ Cattle, hogs, sheep, poultry, and dairy products: milk and cheese

N
W E
S

A French farmer at an outdoor market sells ripe squash and bulbs of garlic straight from his farm.

separate regions, and each has its own special dishes. Yet there is one common thread that ties all French food together: People insist on fresh ingredients.

Freshness is so important to the French that it is not uncommon for people to shop for food every day. Food author Kate Heyhoe explains: "Whereas Americans *avoid* spending time on food, living on diets of Big Macs, Stouffers dinners, and Hamburger Helper, the French devote hours each day just to food *shopping,* especially in Paris. Food is bought fresh daily, from individual merchants."[2] France has supermarkets and many people buy groceries from them. But French cooks prefer shopping in small, specialty markets.

One such market is the **boulangerie**, which sells freshly baked breads. Tantalizing smells fill the air in the boulangerie. In the early morning, before the market is even open, eager customers are lined up outside. They buy flaky, buttery, crescent-shaped rolls called croissants for breakfast. Bread lovers with a sweet tooth may crave pain au chocolat, which is a square pastry with chocolate on the inside.

Also found in most all boulangeries is a long, skinny loaf called a baguette. The French people love baguettes. They eat about 9 billion loaves each year! Meg Cutts, who lives in Paris, describes the perfect baguette: "A real baguette . . . is chewy and soft on the inside and crunchy on the outside. It should feel buttery even if no butter was used in the production. It should beg you to go home right now and get out the soft unsalted butter."[3]

France has special markets for more than just bread. The boucherie, or butcher shop, carries fresh meats, poultry, and game such as wild boar and rabbit. Fat rolls of spicy pork, veal, and garlic sausage are found at the char- cuterie. At the fromagerie, shoppers can find an assort- ment of delicious French cheeses.

French Herb Bread

Baguettes are sold in many grocery stores and some bakeries. This bread is delicious with most any meal.

Ingredients:

3/4 cup butter, at room temperature
3/4 teaspoon each of dried parsley, basil, rosemary, and chives
1/4 teaspoon salt
Pinch of freshly ground black pepper
1 tablespoon grated Gruyère cheese
1 baguette

Instructions:

1. Combine butter with the herbs, salt, pepper, and cheese. Mix well.
2. Heat the oven to 400° F.
3. Use a sharp knife to carefully slice the baguette in half lengthwise.
4. Spread the butter and herb mixture evenly along the cut side of both halves.
5. Bake open face for about six minutes, watching carefully so the bread does not get too brown. Serve hot.

Serves 6 to 8

Working in the early morning hours, a baker at a boulangerie in the village of Darcey prepares baguettes for the oven.

Display cases at the **patisserie** are filled with cakes, sweet pastries, and other mouthwatering desserts.

Fresh from the Farm

French people also flock to open-air markets. These markets are everywhere in France, from the tiniest villages to the largest cities. Once or twice a week, farmers truck in fresh produce that they picked early that same

The French Mystery

French people are thinner and healthier than people in many other countries. This is true even though their meals include multiple courses, and the dishes they eat are often high in fat. The French usually eat what they want. Yet only 11 percent of French adults are obese, compared with more than 30 percent of Americans. Also, the French have some of the lowest cholesterol and heart disease in the world. How could this be? One reason is that food portions are smaller in France. A five-course French meal often has fewer calories than the average American meal has. And unlike many people throughout the world, French people do not snack. If they get hungry in the middle of the day, they might have a cup of hot chocolate or a piece of fresh fruit. Junk food has no place in most French households.

morning. Vendors also sell farm-fresh eggs, cheeses, homemade bread, and herbs and spices. Author Peter Mayle, who lives in the Provence region of France, describes a visit to one of his favorite open-air markets: "[T]he tables were piled high with vegetables, small and fragrant bushes of basil, tubs of lavender honey, great green bottles of first pressing olive oil . . . flowers and herbs, jams and cheeses—everything looked delicious in the early morning sun."[4]

Although produce is available year-round in France, most French people prefer to buy it in season. Mireille Guiliano, who was born and raised in France, explains this preference: "Nothing is more flavorless than a supermarket tomato in winter, but a true vine-ripened specimen in summer is nothing short of divine."[5]

Guiliano says that one of France's most popular fruits is the plum. Known in France as prunes, plums are available in late summer. Some are creamy yellow and no bigger than a cherry tomato. Others are larger and deep purple in color.

The French people love plums so much that they eat about 40 million pounds (18 million kg) every year. They use the fruit in many different ways. They often eat plums raw. They cook the fruit in sugary syrup to make a dessert known as compote. Plums are also baked in buttery crust to make desserts such as tarts.

How to Cook Vegetables

The French enjoy fresh vegetables as much as fruits. The earliest ideas about cooking vegetables may actually have come from France. Religious traditions required that France's large Catholic population not eat meat on many occasions. On these days, the French turned to vegetables. "It is, therefore, from French

Parisians shop for fresh produce at an outdoor market near the Eiffel Tower.

cooks we have derived our happiest directions for cooking vegetables,"[6] writes English cookbook author Ann Bowman.

France's first great food writer, Pierre François del La Varenne, "recorded the first elaborate recipes in which vegetables were the centerpiece,"[7] writes food historian Harold McGee. In *Le Cuisinier françois*, first published in 1651, del La Varenne presents a recipe for "Asparagus in Fragrant Sauce." (His sauce is very much like the modern French hollandaise sauce.) Varenne writes:

> Choose the largest asparagus, scrape them at the bottom, and wash. Cook them in some water, salt them well, and do not let them overcook. When done, let them drain, and make a sauce with some good fresh butter, a little vinegar, salt, and nutmeg, and an egg yolk to bind the sauce; take care that it doesn't curdle. Serve the asparagus well garnished with whatever you like.[8]

Stocks Are Everything

Another way French cooks use vegetables is to make homemade **stocks**. These stocks form the base of many different dishes. Chef Auguste Escoffier, who set the standard for French cooking, wrote about the importance of stocks: "Indeed, stock is everything in cooking, at least in French cooking. Without it, nothing can be done. If one's stock is good, what remains of the work is easy; if, on the other hand, it is bad or merely mediocre, it is quite hopeless to expect anything approaching a satisfactory result."[9]

Brown stock, made from meaty beef bones, vegetables, and seasonings, is used to make glazes for meats. It also forms the base for rich French onion soup. White stock is made from veal, fish, seafood, or poultry. Other ingredients include fresh vegetables, herbs, and white wine. White stock is often used to make thick, creamy chowders.

Glorious Sauces

Stocks are also used to make sauces, which some people consider the heart of French cuisine. This is especially true with elaborate dishes known as **haute cuisine**, which are served in elegant restaurants. Famous cook and author Julia Child referred to sauces as "the splendor and glory of French cooking."[10]

Yet the original use for sauces was quite different. In the days before refrigeration, meat, poultry, and seafood did not last long. To mask the bad flavor of spoiled foods, cooked dishes were smothered in sauces. Today, French sauces are not intended to mask anything. They are used to enhance food and make it taste special.

Wine is used to flavor many sauces. French wines are known as some of the finest in the world, and they are often used in French cooking. One example of a rich wine sauce is **beurre blanc**. It is typically served with lobster, shrimp, and other types of seafood. First, a base is made by combining white wine, shallots (a cousin of the onion), vinegar, and freshly ground pepper. The mixture is boiled for about twenty minutes, or until a small amount of liquid is left in the pan. Then unsalted butter

Two chefs prepare a variety of sauces to go with roasted meat and fish. Stocks and sauces are at the heart of French cuisine.

A Passion for Food

Tomatoes with Goat Cheese

This French dish makes a nice appetizer or substitute for salad.

Ingredients:

6 medium tomatoes
8 ounces goat cheese
1 egg
2 tablespoons olive oil, divided
1 cup dry bread crumbs
1 teaspoon Italian seasoning
$1/2$ teaspoon salt
$1/4$ teaspoon freshly ground black pepper

Instructions:

1. Cut the cores out of the tomatoes and discard. Then slice the top third off of each tomato and save for later use.
2. To help the tomatoes stand up, cut a thin slice off the bottom of each and discard.
3. Use a spoon to carefully scoop out the seeds and pulp and discard.
4. Combine the goat cheese, egg, one tablespoon olive oil, bread crumbs, and seasonings.
5. Heat oven to 400° F.
6. Brush the bottom of an oven-safe casserole dish with the remaining tablespoon of olive oil.
7. Set the tomatoes in the dish.
8. Stuff some of the cheese mixture into each tomato, dividing equally.
9. Put the tops back on the tomatoes, set the casserole dish in the oven, and bake for 20 minutes.

Serve immediately.

A French family gathers outside to enjoy a meal together. A passion for good food and good company is central to French living.

is blended into the boiled mixture and whisked until it is smooth and creamy.

The Joy of Eating

Of all the people in the world, none are more passionate about food than the French. For them, the purpose of eating is much more than just satisfying hunger. A delicious meal shared with family and friends is one of the most enjoyable things in life.

Chapter 2

Bon Appétit!

People in France enjoy and appreciate everything about food: how it looks on the plate, how it smells, and especially how it tastes. Parisian Clotilde Dusoulier shares her perspective: "Every meal should be an extraordinary experience . . . every dish a subtle yet powerful combination of flavors, every bite an explosion of layers to savor."[11]

Savory Fish Stew

Specialty dishes from the various regions in France have been handed down for generations. One is a hearty fish stew known as **bouillabaisse**. Bouillabaisse probably began as a simple soup, made by fisherman on their boats after a long day's work. The soup was

Students at a Parisian cooking school learn how to prepare food that looks as good as it tastes.

most likely made with the catch of the day (or any unsold fish) and a few simple seasonings. It might also have included olive oil, garlic, leeks or onions, and tomatoes.

The village of Marseille is famous for its bouillabaisse. Marseille is located on the Mediterranean Sea, along France's southeast coast. Fresh fish are plentiful there. Each morning, long before the Sun comes up, fishing boats leave Marseille harbor on their way out to sea. The fishermen return four or five hours later and haul in their catch. Peter Mayle describes the scene: "They are there . . . from about eight o'clock each morning, rubber booted and leather faced, standing and shouting behind shallow boxes the size of small dining tables. The catch of the day, often still alive and kicking, shimmers in the sun, silver and gray and blue and red."[12] By the time the fishermen arrive, customers have already lined up on the pier. They

Fishermen in the Mediterranean Sea haul in their catch. Fish are very plentiful in the waters of the Mediterranean.

Quick and Easy Bouillabaisse

This is a simplified version of the famous French fish stew.

Ingredients:

2 large tomatoes, peeled and coarsely chopped
1 green pepper (seeds and core removed), coarsely chopped
1 medium onion, peeled and minced
4 garlic cloves, peeled and finely minced
3 tablespoons olive oil
$1/4$ teaspoon powdered saffron
1 teaspoon salt
$1/2$ teaspoon freshly ground black pepper
2 15-ounce cans beef broth
2 15-ounce cans chicken broth
2 pounds assorted whitefish such as monkfish, red snapper, or ocean perch, cut in 2-inch pieces
$1/2$ pound fresh bay scallops
$1/2$ pound small frozen cooked shrimp, thawed

Instructions:

1. In a large saucepan over medium heat, sauté the tomatoes, pepper, onion, and garlic in olive oil for five to seven minutes, until the onion is soft. Stir in the saffron, salt, and pepper.
2. Add both broths to the sautéed mixture and bring to a boil.
3. Add the whitefish and scallops, cover the pot, and simmer for ten minutes.
4. Add the shrimp and bring the soup to a boil. Serve immediately.

Serves 6 to 8

Bon Appétit!

are eager to look over the fish and select what they need for the day's meals.

French cooks who plan to make bouillabaisse usually buy six or seven kinds of fish. After cleaning it, the heads, tails, and bones are not thrown away. Instead, these trimmings are used to make fish stock, an essential ingredient in bouillabaise. Fish stock is made by boiling the fish trimmings in water with vegetables such as onions and leeks.

When the stock has cooked for four or five hours, it is strained and brought back to a boil. Tomatoes, onions, peppers, and seasonings are sautéed in olive oil and added to the pot. Then the cook adds bite-size pieces of fish such as haddock, whitefish, sea bass, and red snapper.

The last step is to add shellfish. Freshness is so important that shellfish such as lobster, clams, and crabs are often kept alive in a pail of seawater in the kitchen. When it is time to add them, they are dropped right from the pail into the boiling water. The bouillabaisse is cooked for about twenty minutes more. Many French cooks remove the shellfish from the pot before serving the bouillabaisse. The savory broth is ladled into soup bowls over slices of crusty bread. The shellfish is taken to the table on a separate platter.

A Pricey Spice

An essential seasoning in bouillabaisse is a spice called **saffron**. It originated in Asia and was introduced to France in the 1300s. Saffron is either vivid red or yellow, and it is taken from the deep orange stamens of crocus

A vendor at a fish market in Marseille tries to attract customers with the day's catch.

flowers. Because as many as 75,000 crocus blossoms are needed to make a single pound of saffron, it is the world's most expensive spice. Other herbs used in French cooking can be purchased for a fraction of the cost. For example, 1 ounce (28.3g) of basil costs about $3.50 and an ounce of rosemary is $1.25. The same amount of saffron costs more than $100. For that reason, the spice's nickname is "vegetable gold." Because saffron has a very

Harvesters pick threads of red saffron from hundreds of crocus blossoms. Saffron is a key ingredient in bouillabaisse, a popular fish stew.

strong flavor, only a small amount is needed to give bouillabaisse its unique taste.

Pie for Dinner

Another classic French dish is quiche, which is a pie served as a main dish. Quiche is made with pastry, eggs, milk, cream, and cheese. The word *quiche* comes from the German word *küchen*, meaning "cake." The Alsace region of France is often thought to be the home

Saving the Vineyards

Wine is a key ingredient in French cuisine. It is used in sauces, soups, stews, casseroles, and even desserts. French wine is considered some of the best in the world. In the 1860s, however, France's vineyards nearly perished because of a tiny insect known as phylloxera. The phylloxera arrived in France with vine clippings shipped from the United States. The clippings were supposed to give France some new grape varieties. Scientists realized that the American vines had tougher roots and were not harmed by the pests. They grafted the American vine roots onto the French grape vines. The solution worked, and the vineyards of France were saved.

A farmer on a vineyard in Alsace harvests grapes that will be pressed into wine.

of quiche, but it did not begin there. Its roots are actually in a medieval kingdom of Germany known as Lothringen. When the kingdom became part of France, it was renamed Lorraine.

Quiche Lorraine, the original quiche, had a crust made of bread dough. Its filling was made from eggs and cream and dotted with smoked bacon. Today quiche Lorraine is a fancier dish. Its crust is made of buttery, flaky pastry rather than bread dough. The filling is still dotted with bacon, but it is dressed up with chopped ham, green onions, and grated Swiss cheese.

To make quiche, cooks first prepare the pastry. They blend cold pieces of butter with flour and salt until the mixture forms coarse crumbs. Then they stir in ice water to make a dough. They roll the pastry with a rolling pin and carefully fit the pastry into a pie plate or curly-edged (fluted) quiche pan. Then they cut the bacon and ham into small pieces and brown them in a skillet. To make the filling, cooks beat together fresh milk, cream, and eggs with the desired seasonings. Then they arrange the cooked bacon and ham, as well as the finely grated cheese, over the crust in the pan. Finally they pour the filling over the top and bake the quiche in a hot oven.

Puffy Cuisine

Soufflé is another popular French dish. It is light and fluffy, crisp on the outside and creamy in the center. Its name comes from the French word *souffler*, which means

Quiche Lorraine

Ready-made crust works just fine for quiche, and it is much easier than homemade.

Ingredients:

6 slices bacon, chopped
$1/2$ cup cooked ham, chopped
2 tablespoons all-purpose flour
$1/2$ teaspoon salt
$1/8$ teaspoon pepper
3 eggs
1 cup half-and-half
$1/4$ cup chopped green onions
1 ready-made 9-inch pastry shell
4 ounces Swiss or Gruyère cheese, finely grated

Instructions:

1. Brown the chopped bacon and ham in skillet. Drain.
2. In a large bowl combine the flour, salt, and pepper. Add half-and-half and eggs. Beat until smooth. Add green onions.
3. Heat oven to 400° F. Place pastry shell on a baking sheet before filling.
4. Place bacon and ham in the pastry shell.
5. Sprinkle grated cheese over the bacon and ham.
6. Pour the egg mixture over the cheese.
7. Place the quiche in the oven and bake for 30 to 40 minutes, or until golden brown. It is done when a toothpick inserted in the center comes out clean. Let stand about 15 minutes before cutting.

Serves 6 to 8

A chef in Paris drizzles chocolate over a soufflé before placing it in the oven. Sweet soufflés are a very popular French dessert.

"to blow" or "to puff." The description makes perfect sense because soufflés do puff up as they bake.

Soufflés may be either sweet or savory. Sweet soufflés are popular desserts in France. Chocolate soufflé is made with dark, bittersweet chocolate. It may be served with a dusting of powdered sugar or with a thin chocolate sauce. Other favorite sweet soufflés are made with fruits such as raspberries or lemons.

Savory soufflés are usually served as appetizers or light meals. Some are made with vegetables such as chopped fresh mushrooms or **pureed** carrots. Soufflé au poisson, or fish soufflé, is made with steamed cod or salmon. Another popular soufflé is cheese soufflé. Like most savory soufflés, it starts with a sauce known as **béchamel**. Cooks stir together melted butter and flour in a pan to make a thickener known as **roux**. They blend milk into the roux, then add egg yolks and cheese. Finally, they fold in stiffly beaten egg whites. They pour the batter into a buttered, straight-sided earthenware dish and bake the soufflé for 30 to 45 minutes.

Tricky Technique

Soufflés can be tricky to make. Many new cooks have learned the hard way not to peek into the oven while their soufflé is baking. If they do, the soufflé can deflate very quickly. That is because trapped air inside the soufflé causes it to puff up while it is hot. If cool air reaches it, the steam inside the soufflé begins to cool, causing it to collapse.

As soon as a soufflé is removed from the oven, it starts to fall. So, it is served immediately. Some of the outside crust is dished onto serving plates. Then a generous scoop of the creamy center is added to each plate, and the soufflé is served.

Soufflé

A waiter serves a platter of mixed seafood, while a patron prepares to eat a steaming bowl of bouillabaisse at a café in Cassis.

Every region in France has its own mouthwatering cuisine. Some dishes are known only to the local residents, while others have become world famous. By far three of the most famous—and the most delicious—are bouillabaisse, quiche, and soufflé.

Chapter

3

Delicious Desserts

French people love to eat dessert. Some sort of dessert follows most main meals. It is usually chosen based on what was served for the main course. If the main course was heavy, dessert likely will be simple and light. As Mireille Guiliano explains: "American desserts tend to be rich and heavy. . . . In France, we would not have such a dessert following other rich courses. By the same token, not having room for dessert would suggest that the preceding parts of the meal have been too large or too rich."[13]

An Icy, Light Finish

One light, refreshing dessert is **sorbet**, which is the French word for "sherbet." Sorbet is soft and icy and has a silky texture. It is often flavored with fruit or chocolate. Because sorbet does not contain any fat or eggs, it is different from ice cream. For instance, raspberry sorbet contains nothing more than sugar, water, and fresh raspberries.

During the 1800s Auguste Escoffier became especially fond of sorbet. He did not, however, consider it a dessert. He believed it should be served during a meal instead of afterward. Escoffier suggested that main courses be separated by a dish of fruit sorbet. This would cleanse the palate, or clear the taste buds between different types of food. Today sorbet is more commonly served for dessert.

To make sorbet, French cooks start by preparing a syrup. They cook sugar and water until the sugar dis-

A pastry shop in Aix-en-Provence entices passersby with an array of tempting treats.

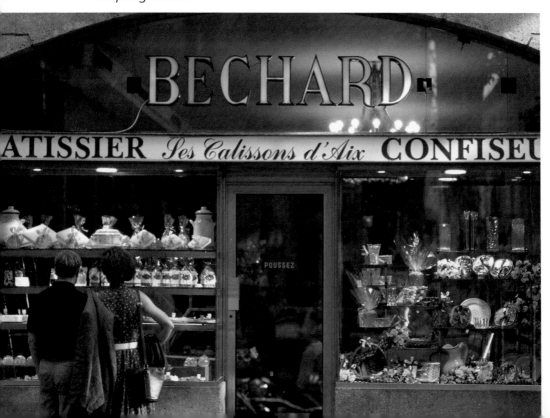

A man serves cones of sorbet from an ice cream shop window in Paris.

solves. Then they add the flavoring. For fruit sorbet, this might be fresh strawberries or peaches that have been whirled in a blender until smooth. Delicious lemon sorbet is made with the juice of fresh lemons. To make chocolate sorbet, cooks add melted bittersweet chocolate instead of fruit.

Once the syrup is ready, cooks set it in the freezer to cool. When it is thoroughly chilled (but not frozen), they place it in an ice cream maker. Paddles churn the sorbet as it freezes. This breaks down the ice crystals and gives the sorbet its velvety smooth texture.

Dessert Crêpes

In France, crêpes are used to make many delicious desserts. Crêpes are extremely thin pancakes filled with sweetened fruit or other fillings.

One of the most elegant French desserts is crêpes Suzette. The crêpes are folded and placed into a heat-proof serving dish. A sauce made from sugar, butter, orange juice, and orange-flavored brandy is heated and then poured over the crêpes. More brandy is poured around them. A match is touched to the liquid, causing it to catch fire. This is all done in full view of guests, and it makes for a dramatic presentation of the flaming dessert.

Crêpes Suzette are thin pancakes stuffed with a sweet filling.

Irresistible Tarts

While light desserts such as sorbet have their place at French tables, France is also famous for its many rich desserts. One example is the tart, which consists of a flaky, buttery pastry and filling. Tarts are one of the most popular desserts in France.

One popular tart is made with fresh peaches. First, cooks prepare the pastry with flour, cold butter, sugar, and ice water. For a delicious nutty flavor, they add ground almonds to the dough. They line a fluted tart pan with the pastry and bake it in a hot oven for about fifteen minutes. Meanwhile, they prepare a filling known as **frangipane**. They mix together butter and sugar, then add eggs and beat the mixture until smooth. They flavor the frangipane with pure almond extract and **kirsch**, a type of brandy made from cherries.

Cooks pour the frangipane into the partially baked crust and arrange sliced fresh peaches over the top. They bake the tart for about 30 minutes, or until the fruit is nicely browned. Then they prepare a glaze. Some make a delicious apricot glaze with apricot preserves and kirsch. They boil the mixture on the stove and then brush it onto the baked tart. The tart is cooled to room temperature before serving.

One of France's most famous tarts is the tarte Tatin. This is a delicious, caramelized upside-down apple pie. The tarte Tatin was invented in the early 1800s, but there are different stories about how it came to be. It began at France's Hotel Tatin, which was owned by sisters Caroline and Stéphane Tatin. The most popular story is that Stéphane was cooking

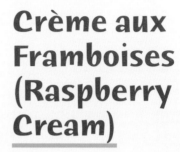

Crème aux Framboises (Raspberry Cream)

Make this lovely, light dessert in the summer when fresh raspberries are in season.

Ingredients:
4 cups fresh raspberries
3 cups heavy cream
1/2 cup granulated sugar

Instructions:
1. Gently wash the raspberries and dry on paper towels .
2. Whirl three cups of the raspberries in a blender or food processor until they are thoroughly crushed.
3. Strain out the seeds with a wire mesh strainer. Use a rubber spatula to push the raspberry puree through the strainer. Discard the seeds.
4. In a large bowl, whip the cream with an electric mixer until soft peaks form. Add sugar and whip just until blended.
5. Gently fold the raspberry puree into the cream.
6. Spoon the mixture into small bowls and garnish with remaining raspberries.
7. Chill in the refrigerator for an hour. Serve cold.

About 6 servings

apples and sugar on the stove to make a tart. She became distracted by a handsome hunter and forgot about the apples. When a caramel scent filled the air, she feared the apples had burned. She needed the tart for her hotel guests, so she laid pastry on top of the skillet of apples and put it into the oven to bake. When the crust had browned, she removed it from the oven and turned it upside down on a platter. It was a strange-looking dessert, but her guests raved about its delicious flavor.

A chef in Alsace slices and marinates various fruits to use as fillings for tarts.

Mouthwatering Custard

France is also famous for its rich **custards**. Custard is creamy and smooth like pudding. How it is cooked depends on the particular dessert. It may be cooked on the stove or baked in the oven.

One baked custard dessert that is especially elegant is crème brûlée. This silky smooth custard is topped with a crackly layer of caramelized sugar. According to food writer Debbie Elkind, the origins of crème brûlée are somewhat fuzzy. She explains: "The Spanish . . . say they invented it during the 18th century. In the south of France, it is known as crème catalan and is believed to have been born there. Meanwhile, the Brits contend that it was first made during the 17th century . . . in Cambridge, where it is known as Cambridge burnt cream or Trinity cream. Indeed, it wasn't until the late 19th century

A favorite French dessert, crème brûlée is a creamy, rich custard topped with a crust of burnt sugar.

that the French translation of 'burnt cream' (crème brûlée) came into vogue, causing the popular perception that it's a uniquely French dish."[14]

To make crème brûlée, cooks heat heavy cream in a saucepan. Then they mix it with sugar, egg yolks, and pure vanilla. They beat the mixture until it is creamy, and pour it into individual serving cups known as **ramekins**. To maintain its smooth consistency, the custard must be baked gently. For this reason, the filled ramekins are placed in a large, shallow pan of hot water. The custard is baked for about 30 minutes. Next, cooks cover the top of each dish with granulated sugar. They then pass a flame over the sugar with a small handheld torch. This causes the sugar to turn brown and bubbly, and the crème brûlée is served immediately.

A French Classic

Custards are also used in luscious pastry desserts such as the **éclair**. Éclairs are made with a type of dough known as **choux paste**. It is an unusual pastry because it is cooked on the stove. Cooks boil butter and water in a saucepan. They stir flour into the mixture and use a wooden spoon to beat the dough. They add eggs one at a time and beat the dough until it is thoroughly mixed. Then they scoop the dough into a pastry tube, which is the same type of tool used to decorate cakes. The tube has a hole in one end so dough can be squeezed, or piped, onto a baking pan. Cooks pipe the dough into oblong shapes. The éclairs are baked until crisp and pale golden in color. During baking, the pastry puffs up and becomes hollow inside.

Chocolate Mousse

This recipe is a delicious and easy version of the rich French dessert.

Ingredients:

8 ounces semisweet chocolate, broken into small pieces
$1/4$ cup granulated sugar
3 egg yolks, beaten
$1 1/4$ cups whipping cream
1 teaspoon pure vanilla
Ready-made whipped cream for topping
Optional: chocolate shavings

Instructions:

1. Place the chocolate pieces in a saucepan that is resting on a pan of hot water. Stir until the chocolate is melted.
2. Add the sugar to the chocolate and mix well.
3. Beat the egg yolks in a small bowl. Stir about a tablespoon of the hot mixture into the beaten egg yolks. Blend thoroughly, then pour the yolks back into the chocolate and mix well.
4. Cook, stirring constantly, until the mixture has thickened. Remove from heat, stir in the vanilla, and allow to cool.
5. In a large bowl, beat the whipping cream with an electric mixer until soft peaks form.
6. Fold the cooled chocolate mixture into the whipping cream and gently blend.
7. Spoon the mixture into four ramekins and set them in the refrigerator.
8. After the mousse has cooled, top each dish with a dollop of the ready-made whipped cream and serve.

Serves 4

A chef squeezes choux paste onto a tray to form éclairs, the heavenly pastries filled with custard.

Meanwhile, cooks prepare the custard filling. They simmer a mixture of milk, egg yolks, cornstarch, and sugar on the stove until thick. They cover the pot and allow it to cool for about an hour. Then they gently fold whipped cream in, along with a kiss of pure almond flavoring. To assemble the éclairs, the cooks use a sharp knife to slit the side of each pastry. Then they use a pastry tube to pipe in the custard filling. Just before serving, they drizzle dark chocolate icing over the top of each éclair.

A counter in a Paris restaurant displays a variety of desserts, including a fruit cup, muffins, and a fruit tart.

In France, dessert is a favorite part of the meal—and French desserts are some of the finest in the world. From light and icy sorbets to mouthwatering tarts, from cream-filled éclairs to rich crème brûlée, the desserts from France are nothing short of irresistible.

Chapter 4

Foods for Celebrating

Holidays in France are wonderful and exciting. French people love food and love to celebrate. That is why, as Clotilde Dusoulier explains, "Every celebration is always tied in with food and drink."[15]

Christmas Feast

The Christmas season, known as Noel, is a magical time in France. About mid-November, twinkling lights begin to appear on trees in towns and villages, as well as in the windows of homes and shops. French cooks eagerly plan their holiday menus and shop for the ingredients they will need. They make a wide variety of delicious foods.

In the Provence region of France, Christmas Eve is a time of great celebration. It is traditional for two dinners

A Christmas market in Alsace sells foods that French families typically enjoy on Christmas Eve.

to be served. The first, known as le petit souper (small supper), is served early in the evening. Writer Michele Serre describes a typical menu for such a meal: "[C]hicken soup swimming with big lacy noodles, a fine codfish fried with onions and olives, a capon or nice plump goose stuffed with truffles or prunes, accompanied by a gratin of Swiss chard [a type of beet] cooked in the oven with the poultry juices, a winter salad sprinkled with garlic croutons, and a squash pie."[16] The early meal lasts for several hours. Family members talk, laugh, listen to holiday music, and share their favorite stories.

After attending a midnight church service, family members arrive back home. They are served a second meal that is even bigger than the first one was. It is known as le gros souper (grand supper). The meal is an elaborate French feast. Squash soup is the traditional first course. The second course is typically escargots (snails), that

The French often eat in the company of family and friends. Holidays, in particular, are occasions for festive family gatherings.

have been cooked in broth with tomato and garlic. Other traditional courses include fried onions, vegetables such as cauliflower and artichokes in olive oil, and a salad made of fresh, crisp greens such as endive.

The crowning glory of le gros souper is dessert—and it is actually thirteen desserts. Most people believe the number thirteen was chosen in honor of Jesus and his twelve apostles. The dessert courses consist of dried fruits such as figs, prunes, and raisins, as well as almonds, hazelnuts, and walnuts. Nougat, which is a traditional

Celebrating Snails!

People in France do not need official holidays in order to celebrate. They love food so much that they hold festivals to honor it. One example is snails, or escargots, which are a popular French delicacy. More than 40,000 tons (36,287 metric tons) of snails are eaten in France every year! And each July, snails are honored at an event known as Foire aux Escargots ("celebration of the snail"). It is held in the town of Martigny-les-Bains, and thousands of people attend. There is a parade during which a queen (Miss Coquille, which means "shell") is crowned. After the festivities, there are plenty of buttery, garlicky escargots for everyone's eating pleasure.

Petits Fours de Noel

These cinnamon butter cookies are a traditional Christmas favorite in France's Alsace region.

Ingredients:
2 cups all-purpose flour
$3/4$ teaspoon baking powder
1 cup powdered sugar
1 teaspoon ground cinnamon
Grated rind of $1/2$ lemon
$3/4$ cup butter, at room temperature
3 eggs

Instructions:
1. In a large bowl, sift together the flour, baking powder, powdered sugar, and cinnamon. Stir in the grated lemon rind.
2. In a separate bowl, combine the butter with two of the eggs and beat well.
3. Combine flour and creamed mixtures. Mix well.
4. Cover and refrigerate for eight hours (or overnight).
5. Heat the oven to 350° F.
6. On a lightly floured surface, use a rolling pin to roll the dough to a thickness of one-quarter inch.
7. Cut the dough into desired shapes with cookie cutters.
8. Spray baking sheets with nonstick cooking spray and carefully place the cutouts on them.
9. Separate the remaining egg and discard the white. Beat the yolk with one tablespoon water. Brush this mixture over the top of each cookie.
10. Bake for twelve to fifteen minutes, or until golden brown.

Makes about 3 dozen

French candy made with almonds and honey, is another of the desserts. Fresh fruits such as mandarin oranges, apples, and pears are often served, as are Provençal grapes still attached to their stems. Other desserts may include cakes, fruit tarts, and assorted candies.

The Hidden Charm of Epiphany

A few weeks after Noel, another holiday is celebrated in France. L'Epiphanie, which means "the epiphany," was

A chef ladles melted chocolate into a mold to make the hollow chocolate eggs (inset) that children receive during Easter.

originally a religious holiday. It marked the visit of the Three Kings to the baby Jesus twelve days after his birth. For some people in France, l'Epiphanie has lost much of its religious meaning. Still, it is a time for celebrating.

As far back as the 1500s, France celebrated l'Epiphanie with a dessert known as the Twelfth Night cake. A bean or tiny ceramic figure was baked inside it. Whoever discovered the prize in his or her slice became "royalty" for the day. Many French families still practice this ritual. Their traditional dessert is known as galette des rois. It is a buttery pastry with rich, smooth almond-flavored filling. People may bake their own galette des rois from scratch, or buy one at the local patisserie. French pastry chef Jean-Luc Albian describes the special holiday ritual: "In most areas of France, a tiny plastic king or queen is baked into the galette des rois, but in some rural towns you can still find the little ceramic toys and animals that have been inserted in the cakes for hundreds of years."[17]

Easter Sweets and Lamb

In the spring of each year, another holiday is celebrated in France. It is called Pâques, which means "Easter." Children eagerly anticipate Pâques because they receive a special treat: a hollow chocolate shell shaped like an egg, duck, hen, or rabbit. Inside is an assortment of delicious chocolates and other candies.

A traditional Easter dish, legs of lamb covered with several different kinds of herbs, cook slowly over a coal fire.

The traditional main course for Pâques dinner is roast leg of lamb. Because lambs are born in the spring, feasting on lamb was seen as a way of welcoming the spring season.

Cooks prepare this dish in many different ways. One delicious recipe calls for the lamb to be roasted with garlic, rosemary, dried lavender, and orange peel. The day before Easter, cooks make small slits in the lamb and insert slices of fresh garlic. Then they blend olive oil, salt, freshly ground pepper, lavender, and orange peel in a mixing bowl and whisk it until smooth. They rub the meat with the savory mixture, and then cover and refrigerate it overnight. The next morning, they remove the dish from the refrigerator and allow it to sit at room temperature for a few hours. Then they place the seasoned lamb on a metal rack in a roasting pan and bake it in the oven for about an hour. After roasting, cooks carve the lamb into long, thin slices. It is often served with spring vegetables such as fresh, crisp asparagus or small green peas. Other courses might be a bubbling potato casserole, green salad, an assortment of cheeses, and dessert.

Bastille Day Picnics

Lavender

Another time for celebration in France is July 14. Sometimes called Bastille Day, most French simply call it le 14 juillet. It marks the day in 1789 when French revolutionaries seized the Bastille prison. That signaled the beginning of the French Revolution. It was a major step in France's freedom from the oppressive rule of King Louis XVI and his queen, Marie Antoinette. Le 14 juillet is celebrated as France's independence day, much like July 4 is celebrated in the United States.

Picnickers in the town of Sully sur Loire celebrate Bastille Day with lunch in front of an old castle.

Le 14 juillet is an exciting time. There are military parades, dancing in the streets, and elaborate fireworks. Families pack lunches and enjoy picnics along riverbanks, and even right in the center of town. In the spirit of the holiday, however, menus are kept simple. Before the French Revolution, many people in France starved while royalty lived lavishly in their castles. For this reason, the French tradition during le 14 juillet is to avoid splurging on extravagant meals.

Holiday picnic baskets are filled with such foods as fresh-baked baguettes, cold roasted chicken, vegetable

Cold Peach and Strawberry Soup

This delicious cold soup is easy to make. It is perfect for the French holiday le 14 juillet.

Ingredients:

6 medium-size peaches
4 cups water
1 cup granulated sugar
1^1/$_2$ pounds fresh strawberries
1 cup powdered sugar
1 teaspoon fresh lemon juice

Instructions:

1. Peel the peaches. Cut in half to remove pits. Dice.
2. In a saucepan combine the water and granulated sugar. Boil.
3. Add the diced peaches. Simmer for ten minutes.
4. Remove the pan from the heat and drain the peaches, saving the liquid.
5. In a food processor or blender, puree the strawberries, powdered sugar, and lemon juice until smooth, about two to three minutes.
6. Combine the strawberry mixture with the peach liquid. Bring it to a boil.
7. Reduce the heat and simmer for ten minutes, or until the mixture is reduced by one-third.
8. Spoon the cooked peaches into bowls and ladle the raspberry mixture over the top. Chill before serving.

Serves 4

casseroles, and cold fruit soups. Other popular foods include crisp green salads, spicy sausage, sautéed olives, fruit, and a variety of cheeses.

One salad that is popular for le 14 juillet picnics is salad niçoise. It is made with fresh vegetables and canned white tuna. To prepare it, cooks toss salad greens with the tuna. Then they add sliced cooked potatoes, cherry tomatoes, red and green pepper strips, radishes, hard-boiled eggs, and black olives. Then they pour a salad dressing known as vinaigrette over the salad. The dressing is made with olive oil, three kinds of vinegar, chopped shallots, seasonings, and Dijon mustard.

In France, people are known for their joie de vivre, which means "joy of life." Holidays are always special, happy times to be shared among family and friends. From elaborate dinners during Noel to riverbank picnics during le 14 juillet, the French believe that food and celebrations naturally go together.

Metric Conversions

Mass (weight)

1 ounce (oz.)	= 28.0 grams (g)
8 ounces	= 227.0 grams
1 pound (lb.) or 16 ounces	= 0.45 kilograms (kg)
2.2 pounds	= 1.0 kilogram

Liquid Volume

1 teaspoon (tsp.)	= 5.0 milliliters (ml)
1 tablespoon (tbsp.)	= 15.0 milliliters
1 fluid ounce (oz.)	= 30.0 milliliters
1 cup (c.)	= 240 milliliters
1 pint (pt.)	= 480 milliliters
1 quart (qt.)	= 0.95 liters (l)
1 gallon (gal.)	= 3.80 liters

Pan Sizes

8-inch cake pan	= 20 x 4-centimeter cake pan
9-inch cake pan	= 23 x 3.5-centimeter cake pan
11 x 7-inch baking pan	= 28 x 18-centimeter baking pan
13 x 9-inch baking pan	= 32.5 x 23-centimeter baking pan
9 x 5-inch loaf pan	= 23 x 13-centimeter loaf pan
2-quart casserole	= 2-liter casserole

Length

1/4 inch (in.)	= 0.6 centimeters (cm)
1/2 inch	= 1.25 centimeters
1 inch	= 2.5 centimeters

Temperature

212° F	= 100° C (boiling point of water)
225° F	= 110° C
250° F	= 120° C
275° F	= 135° C
300° F	= 150° C
325° F	= 160° C
350° F	= 180° C
375° F	= 190° C
400° F	= 200° C

Notes

Chapter 1: A Passion for Food

1. Quoted in Mimi Spencer, "Let Them Eat Cake," *Observer*, November 7, 2004. http://observer.guardian.co.uk/foodmonthly/story/0,9950,1342296,00.html.
2. Kate Heyhoe, "Foie Gras in France," *Kate's Global Kitchen*, December 25, 1999. www.globalgourmet.com/food/kgk/1299/kgk122599.html.
3. Meg Cutts, "Best Little Bakery in Paris," *Too Many Chefs*, February 22, 2004. www.toomanychefs.net/archives/2004_02.php.
4. Peter Mayle, *A Year in Provence*. New York: Vintage Books, 1991, p. 72.
5. Mireille Guiliano, *French Women Don't Get Fat*. New York: Alfred A. Knopf, 2005, p. 71.
6. Quoted in Harold McGee, *On Food and Cooking: The Science and Lore of the Kitchen*. New York: Charles Scribner's Sons, 1984, p. 132.
7. McGee, *On Food and Cooking*, p. 133.
8. Quoted in McGee, *On Food and Cooking*, p. 133.
9. Auguste Escoffier, *The Escoffier Cookbook*. New York: Crown, 1969, p. 1.
10. Julia Child, Louisette Bertholle, and Simone Beck, *Mastering the Art of French Cooking*. New York: Alfred A. Knopf, 1969, p. 54.

Chapter 2: Bon Appétit!

11. Clotilde Dusoulier, *Chocolate & Zucchini,* September 29, 2003. http://chocolateandzucchini.com.
12. Peter Mayle, *Encore Provence: New Adventures in the South of France.* New York: Vintage Books, 2000, p. 89.

Chapter 3: Delicious Desserts

13. Guiliano, *French Women Don't Get Fat,* p. 142.
14. Debbie Elkind, "Burnt Offerings," *Sydney Morning Herald,* August 30, 2003. www.smh.com.au/articles/2003/08/29/1062050662479.html.

Chapter 4: Foods for Celebrating

15. Clotilde Dusoulier, online interview with the author, February 21, 2005.
16. Michele Serre, "Flavors of France," *The Worldwide Gourmet.* www.theworldwidegourmet.com/holidays/christmas/provence.htm.
17. Quoted in "History of the French King Cake," *Maurice French Pastries.* www.mauricefrenchpastries.com/html/french_king_cakes.html.

Glossary

béchamel: A basic white sauce made with butter, flour, and milk.

beurre blanc: A buttery French sauce.

boulangerie: A French bakery that specializes in different types of bread.

bouillabaisse: A savory fish stew.

choux paste: A type of pastry that is cooked in a saucepan before it is baked.

custards: Creamy desserts that are either cooked on the stove or baked.

éclair: A French pastry filled with custard and drizzled with chocolate icing.

frangipane: A filling that is often used to make fruit tarts.

haute cuisine: The most elegant of all French cooking.

kirsch: A type of brandy made from cherries.

patisserie: A French pastry shop.

pureed: Strained or blended until smooth.

ramekins: Small individual serving dishes.

roux: A thickener used to make sauces.

saffron: A pungent (and expensive) yellow spice made from crocus flowers.

sorbet: A velvety-smooth frozen dessert.

stocks: Savory broths made by boiling meat and/or bones with vegetables and herbs.

For Further Exploration

Books

Rosalba Gioffrè, *The Young Chef's French Cookbook (I'm the Chef)*. New York: Crabtree, 2001. Includes a variety of recipes as well as information about French food, culture, geography, holidays, and festivals.

Sue Townsend, *France (World of Recipes)*. Chicago: Heinemann Library, 2002. A collection of recipes for French appetizers, main courses, and desserts, plus cultural and nutritional information.

Lynne Marie Waldee, *Cooking the French Way (Easy Menu Ethnic Cookbooks)*. Minneapolis: Lerner, 2002. Includes many recipes and photographs, as well as step-by-step instructions.

Web Sites

Cool Planet (www.oxfam.org.uk/coolplanet/onthe line/explore/journey/france/frindex.htm). This is a wonderful online guidebook to France that includes a section on French food.

France for Kids (www.ambafrance-us.org/kids). A great site presented by the French embassy that features information on French history and geography, life in France, games, and a French language tutorial.

Index

Albian, Jean-Luc, 49
Alsace region, 24, 26
appetizers, 16, 29
asparagus, 13

baguettes, 7, 8
Bastille Day picnics, 51–54
béchamel sauce, 29
beurre blanc, 14, 17
boucheries (butcher shops), 7
bouillabaisses, 18, 20–24
boulangeries (bread bakeries), 7
Bowman, Ann, 11, 13
breads, 7, 8
breakfast foods, 7
burnt cream, 38–39

cakes, 49
cheese
  in appetizers, 16
  in quiche, 24, 26, 27
  shops, 7
  in soufflés, 29
Child, Julia, 14
chocolate
  for Easter, 49
  mousse, 40
  in pastries, 7
  in sorbets, 32, 33
  in soufflés, 28
cholesterol, 10
Christmas foods, 43–48
cookies, 47
crème aux framboises

(raspberry cream), 36
crème brûlée, 38–39
crêpes, 34
crocus flowers, 22–23
croissants, 7
Cuisinier françois, Le (del La Varenne), 13
custards, 38–39, 41
Cutts, Meg, 7

del La Varenne, Pierre François, 13
desserts
  chocolate mousse, 40
  for Christmas dinners, 46–48
  crème aux framboises, 36
  crêpes, 34
  custards, 38–39
  éclairs, 39, 41
  for Epiphany, 49
  main course and, 31
  sorbet, 31–33
  soufflés, 28
  tarts, 34–35, 37
Dusoulier, Clotilde, 18, 43

Easter foods, 49–51
éclairs, 39, 41
Elkind, Debbie, 38–39
Epiphany food, 48–49
escargots (snails), 45–46
Escoffier, Auguste, 13, 32, 33

fat, in food, 10, 32, 33
fish
  soufflé, 29
  stew, 18, 20–24
Foire aux Escargots food, 46
food, freshness of, 6–7, 9–11, 20, 22
14 juillet picnics, le, 51–54
frangipane, 35
fromageries (cheese shops), 7
fruit
  for Christmas dinners, 46
  in crème aux framboises, 36
  in crêpes, 34
  for 14 juillet picnics, 53
  plums, 11
  in sorbets, 32, 33
  in soufflés, 28
  in tarts, 35, 37

galette des rois (Twelfth Night cake), 49
goat cheese, 16
gros souper, le (grand supper), 45–48
Guiliano, Mireille, 11

haute cuisine, 14
health, 10
heart disease, 10
herbs, 8

Heyhoe, Kate, 6–7
holiday foods
  for Bastille Day, 51–54
  for Christmas, 43–48
  for Easter, 49–51
  for Epiphany, 48–49
  for Foire aux
    Escargots, 46
Hotel Tatin, 35

independence day, 51

junk food, 10

lamb, 50–51
L'Hermite, Françoise, 4
Lorraine, 26
Lothringnen, 26
Louis XVI (king of
  France), 51

Marie Antoinette
  (queen of France), 51
Marseille, 20
Martigny-les-Bains, 46
Mayle, Peter, 10–11, 20
meals, pleasure and, 4,
  17
meat
  for Easter, 50–51
  glazes for, 14
  in Quiche Lorraine, 27
  shops for, 7

Noel foods, 43–48
nougat, 46–48

obesity, 10
open-air markets, 9–11

pain au chocolat, 7
Pâques foods, 49–51
pastries
  chocolate, 7

éclairs, 39, 41
galette des rois
  (Twelfth Night cake),
  49
patisseries (bakeries), 9
peaches, 35, 53
petits fours de Noel, 47
petit souper, le (small
  supper), 44–45
phylloxera, 25
portion sizes, 10
Provence, 43–48
prunes, les (plums), 11

quiche, 24, 26, 27

raspberries, 36
recipes
  asparagus, 13
  bouillabaisses, 21
  chocolate mousse, 40
  crème aux
    framboises, 36
  herb bread, 8
  petits fours de Noel,
    47
  Quiche Lorraine, 27
  tomatoes with goat
    cheese, 16
roux, 29

saffron, 22–24
salads, 16, 54
sauces, 14, 17, 29
savory soufflés, 29
seasonings, 22–24
Serre, Michele, 44–45
shellfish, 21, 22
snacks, 10
snails, 45–46
sorbet (sherbet), 31–33
soufflés, 26, 28–29
soups
  bases for, 14

bouillabaisses, 18,
  20–24
for Christmas
  dinners, 44, 45, 46
for 14 juillet picnics,
  53
spices, 22–24, 51, 54
stews, 18, 20–24
stocks
  fish, 22
  importance of, 13
  uses for, 14
strawberries, 53
sweet soufflés, 28

tarte Tatin, 35, 37
tarts, 34–35, 37
Tatin, Caroline, 35
Tatin, Stéphane, 35, 37
tomatoes
  in bouillabaisse, 21,
    22
  with goat cheese, 16
Twelfth Night cake, 49

vegetable gold, 23
vegetables
  in bouillabaisse, 21,
    22
  for Christmas
    dinners, 44, 45, 46
  cooking, 11, 13
  for Easter dinners, 51
  for 14 juillet picnics,
    54
  in soufflés, 29
  tomatoes, 16
vinaigrettes, 54
vineyards, 25

weight, 10
wine
  importance of, 25
  in sauces, 14, 17

Picture Credits

About the Author

Peggy J. Parks holds a bachelor of science degree from Aquinas College in Grand Rapids, Michigan, where she graduated magna cum laude. She has written more than 40 titles for Thomson Gale's KidHaven Press, Blackbirch Press, and Lucent Books imprints and has also written and self-published her own cookbook. Parks lives in Muskegon, Michigan, a town she says inspires her writing because of its location on the shores of Lake Michigan.